IN SEARCH OF A BAUL WARBLER

ALAK PAL

Made with ❤ on the Notion Press Platform
www.notionpress.com

To my daughter Dew,

Time never ran short for her

when it came listening to my

poems even in the rush of

thousands of her work.

Contents

Contents

Contents

IN SEARCH OF A BAUL WARBLER

• ix •

Foreword

The Bengali volume of these Poems has long been published and cordially welcomed by the Bengali readers throughout the globe. I feel extremely privileged to add a few words to the English version of the book of poem. Its creator Dr. Alak Pal has imparted a selection of the real language of man in a state of vivid sensation and that sort of pleasure by fitting a metrical arrangement, which a Poet may rationally endeavour to impart. The principal object proposed in these Poems was to choose incidents and situations from common life, and to relate them, throughout, as far as was possible in a selection of language really used by common men and at the same time, to throw over them a certain colouring of imagination, whereby ordinary things should be presented to the mind in an unusual aspect; and, further, and above all, to make these incidents and situations interesting by tracing in them, truly though not ostentatiously, the primary laws of our nature. Humble and rustic life was generally chosen, because, in that condition, the essential passions of the heart find a better soil in which they can attain their maturity, are less under restraint and speak a plainer and more emphatic language, because in that condition of life our elementary feelings coexist in a state of greater simplicity and consequently may be more accurately contemplated and more forcibly communicated. I would like to emphasize here that each of these poems has a purpose, which distinguishes these Poems from the popular Poetry of the day. I have carried the Bengali book about with me for days to understand the inner meaning of the poems and our beloved Poet is prompt in replying if any of his readers write to him about the ideas he poured in the book. Some of the lyrics are full of subtlety of rhythm, of untranslatable delicacies of colour and of metrical invention. Dr. Pal is so abundant, so spontaneous, so daring in his passion, so full of surprise, because he is doing something which has never seemed strange, unnatural, or in need of defense. The use of allusion, diction, metaphor, imagery and personification in his poetry shows that though a physician by profession, Dr. Alak Pal is a gifted Poet. He has written in a highly individualistic way, developing his own private mythology through the use of keywords and symbols weaving together themes and images in ways that are not always immediately obvious to the reader and so Dr. Pal has often been seen as a 'Difficult Poet'. Many of the studies of his writings seek to make connections with episodes of his life and it is certainly true that on one level, Dr. Alak Pal was a strongly autobiographical Poet. His is a poetry about searching for identity. The poems are not analysed so much as keys to a life, rather as readings that focus on Pal's artistry and skills as a writer, relying on many of his own statements about the nature and meaning of writing. In one of his poems he brings Abhumanyu, a character foregrounded from the Mahabharata, was the discovery of an explosive new talent. Here we see a rebel, who would brook no constraints on his poetic imagination, no limits on his artistic apparatus. Last but not the least, it has been found by many that poetry can act as medicine. This connection between poetry and medicine has been made for centuries–indeed it can be found in ancient mythology too. Pal's poetry does not make us weaker, never lulls us to sleep, but they strike us to wake from reverie and confront the truth. The Poet teaches us that one cannot sleep peacefully in which world 'youth grows pale, and spectre-thin and dies'. Know not whether poetry opened his to ask patients the right questions or not but, his poetry will definitely help all the readers to overcome their stresses, superstitions and fatigue, especially in their formative years. Pal's poetry does a better job in teaching because it is about embracing the human aspect of suffering, not just knowing how many lymph nodes are positive and where the pain is on a 1-to-10 scale. I know not, Dr. Alak Pal worked harder at being a poet or a physician but through his career trajectory so far, he excelled at both.

Riddhi Mukhopadhyay

1. In Search Of A Baul Warbler

What did you say ? Baul Warbler ?
No, I never heard of a bird
With such name
Are you sure ? Its Baul Warbler ?
Aren't you mixing it up
With Babui bird ?
I see, it's Baul Warbler
Is it an indigenous one
Found in our country ?
If one looks for it with all his heart
And if the luck favours
One might have a glimpse of a Baul Warbler.

Wait - let me open a
Bengali dictionary
Yes, now I got it -
Baul songs, Baul religion
Baul fair, Baul mind …
But no
It does not say anything of
The Baul Warbler.
Have you ever seen

This Baul Warbler ?
Oh, you too haven't seen it.
Searching for long !

So long the thing is
No book, no movie
Or no canvas of an artist
Carry any image of this Baul Warbler
That being the case,
If you clap eyes
On this Baul Warbler one day
How would you concede it?
As you have gone through not even a picture of this passerine.

What did you say ?
Tiny possibility is there that you have a glimpse of the Baul
Warbler
And if it falls upon your sight out of the blue
You will not err in discerning the bird.

O dear ! You have simply thrown me a riddle
Wrapped in a mystery inside an enigma,
A peculiar fret has raised
In my mind too
As I talked to you
I feel a weird craving to see your Baul Warbler.

Be kind
To let me know
If you ever
Get trace of the Baul Warbler.
Loads of thanks to you.

2. Here Until Now

Here until now the night intensifies
Horse of hush tiptoes stealthily
Numb is the chest of the wind trembles very slow
Clouds be the custodian of the chaste moon.

The winter fog lingers here until now,
Unknown cart emits smoke in the distant signal
Fluffy snows pile up in the stations
Playing with doubts and suspicions.

Here until now the sky is gray and dim,
Storms perhaps prepare to pour in
The sand under the cedars are slipping
As morale of broken mind slowly disappears.

Juvenile soul strings the Gandiva
Reluctant to accept the certain vanquish.
He bears Abhimanyu's blood in his veins
And determined to keep the bet once.

Slumber did not visit their eyes for many a days,
Dreaming a dreaming is an extravagance here.
Virtue is sacrificed here in the cycle of luxury,

Even the Supreme Father never thought this will happen someday.

Here until now the time awaits moving.
Waiting will remain on for a measured cadence,
In the greenroom surrounded with closed eyelids,
We must meet in some other name.

3. Today's Abhimanyu

Like a chariot pulled by seven horses
The sound of the first tram at the dawn
Goes rubbing his chest
And Abhimanyu wakes up —
Tightening the worn out leather belt
Upon the loose pants
Around his waist
Abhimanyu leaves for the battlefield.
None taught him
The art of the warfare,
Neither is there any infallible arrow of victory
In his Gandiva.
Nor there is the excitement of a returning victorious
In his discourse.

Since morning to evening
He moves forward
Pushing the stream of crowd,
He gets back again
Pushing the same crowd.

Another day ends
Ends another battle,

Blood transforms itself into sweat
When today's Abhimanyu
Retires to his grimy bed.

· 7 ·

The wearied body
Sleeps quietly
Until the chariot pulled by seven horses
Runs through his chest.

4. Mother Of Seven Offspring

Mother of Seven Offspring
Third and fifth are no more
Your despair is probably lesser but
Than Bhanumati living in the neighbourhood of the
potters—

Her only daughter
Washed away in the inundation;
Hence her agony
Is greater than yours.

Mother of seven offspring
Before crossing the tender age of girlhood
You were married merely at sixteen
Burdened in family life
Like a blinkered oxen.
But your dejection is not the loftiest.

Just think of the youngest daughter in law
Of the house where you work
She teaches in an English medium school
But in spite she strove a lot

Could not be a mother
Her despair is
Much much more than yours.

Your kitchen cries
For a morsel of food every single day
Your Sharee is cleft with
Time's large dents
You knot them to drape around your waist
You are not to be sad
Being bereft of your third and fifth

You cannot estimate
How fortunate you are!
You don't need to feed
Two more mouths

Your frame is
As impregnable as copper
Your mind has long lost dreams
Of a petal strewn bed
You need not visit schools and colleges
To acquire knowledge
About how to endure patiently

For you only envy
That all possess in their minds

'Cause despite you lost your third and fifth
You are the Mother of Seven Offspring
Your anguish and your despair
Your agony
Is much much lesser
Than the other.
Am I not absolutely right
Mother of Seven Offspring ?

5. The Islands

Dispersed, disbanded and scattered people
Are like the outlying and isolated islands
They have much of a muchness but distinct as well
All hide their wounds within themselves.

Salt decayed wall plaster
Of the house
Will gradually be disappear
Unknowingly in diluvium.
Living in a great pride
With the prosperity of tomorrow
Keeping all comforts aside
For the future.

Thought of chaining the time
Is no doubt absurd
Is there anyone with a wide heart
Who could provide refuge by embracing tight !

There is not much difference
Between broader day and profound night
As all sleep and awake
With the touch of neon lamps.

The floating of the dispersed, disbanded and scattered people
Who are like the outlying and isolated islands -
Are chased even today
By Behula of the destiny of time.

6. Nobody Holds His Horse

Nobody holds his horse
Neither the sunny morning
Nor the sky of the autumn
Mossy soil brings with it a fragrance
If got drenched somewhere.
All go back
Nobody holds his horse.

You imagine that
One day time will come
When you'll stand beneath the sky holding your eyes up
Pleasing colours of joy
Would pass their fingers upon the canvas
Subtly where needed ;
But time does not wait
Time is not a rented cab
That it would wait
Only if the price of the meter is paid.
Though there are a few
Who wait without caring for time
They hold their horse
As dock waits

For the anchoring of ship,
Parents wait
For their children's home coming,
Arid fields
Wait for the rain of Bhadra
And the sleepless gloomy night
Wait for the dawn.

7. Merely A Dream

First came the men, stealthily
One after another–
Like a pavid doe.
They take a glance all around
And draw a fringe of Lakshmana
Around the place.

They fly in the air
A handful of saffron soil
From north to south
And sand, dust - all disappeared.

The thumb of their feet
Softly touch the river water
As transparent as crystal
Whose face reflects into it ?
And then hero and heroine exit
Before one can catch a glimpse of them.
Taking a posy of green grass
Between the two palms
In an endeavour to fade the colour by rubbing hard
And a chest full of breathe
Reminiscences of the previous birth.

First came the men
Dreams came much much later
Gradually the dreams smidgen
Centering the men.

Inspissated dreams
Almost like the reality
Grapples the men, who are like a group of islands
Scattered here and there.
But one day
These men cross the fringe of Lakshmana
They blotch their forehead with the saffron soil
And get back one after another
To their homes.
Skeletons of the vision
Look blandly
It is incredible to imagine
Being bereft of the men
They are simply living
As the dreams.

8. The Words I Failed To Keep

I was confident enough while assuring Ma
That I shall get back in the Poush Mela this year
I'll certainly come home
Keeping aside the want of bed
I shall tuck a chuddar upon the stubbles
And the entire family will enjoy the biting cold
Surrendering ourselves under a single quilt.
We together will crisp-bake the winter through our own warmth.

After that so many winters came about
And deserted the remains of leaves of Shal, earthen pots
In the broken Poush Mela
My homecoming did not occur.

I adjured to Sumana that we shall
Come face to face on the day of Dol Yatra in Santiniketan
I thought to make a plan in such a way like
We have met by chance
Beneath the Shimul plant.
Then we shall be lost in ourselves
Ignoring the entire world,

And I shall proffer the saffron Abeer in my hand
To her parting of hair.

The day of Dol Yatra comes every year
Colour of Abeer is still saffron
Although the parting of Sumana's hair
Is colourless until today.

In the inflated state of
The river Kopai in the month of Bhadra
In the kayak made of the trunk of a palm tree
Does Bhombal still bide his time for me?
Does he still anticipate if I reach all of a sudden
By the last train of the night ?

At the close of the day in the month of Falgun
Upon the patio of the temple
In the hazy light of lantern
The boys of the open - air theatre of Notun Gram
Wait for me with their long drawn shadows
I gave them words that
I shall be the prompter of their new performance.
They have not yet started their show in my absence
And I could not keep my words.

Oh, the chillness of the month of Poush
The Dol and Abeer of Falgun

Swollen river of Bhadra, overflowing its shore
And the earthen lamp of the temple -
All your memories get accumulated
In the wicker hut which shelters
Numerous words which I failed to keep.

I love to imagine
Probably there is time
One day perhaps
I shall empty
The wicker hut that shelters
Numerous words which I failed to keep.

9. Cactus

Eighty-seven sits dizzily at the balcony
Stricken with drowsiness-
After breaking his lumbar spine
He is now decrepit and inert
His demeanour is pervaded with disappointment
Cactus of envy pricks within his mind
When he thinks of Seventy-two.

Listening to the news of ten at night
And putting off all the lights of each and every room
Seventy-two comes
And lies down straight on bed.
Is lonesome and solitary-
And feels as if there is some sand of envy
Within the closed eyelids
Meant for Fifty-three.

Watching a movie
At the last show of night
The two entire a Chinese restaurant
They finish their dinner with hakka noodle
And then chewed sweet beetle.
Merry in mood Fifty-three heads towards home

Humming a film song.

In a sudden blow of a motor bike
A tremendously prompt gust of wind
Runs touching his two ears
Fifty-three feels the fragrance of jasmine
Which fill up his nostrils to the brim-Embracing the waist of
Thirty-two
Pressing her melons tight at his back
Twenty-nine gloriously settles down
At the back seat of the bike.
Thirty - two is at unrest
Twenty - nine will get down from his bike
After a little while
A milk - white Mercedes is waiting for her
In the shopping mall;
Her hubby, an employee of a multinational company
Owns this fabulous car.

Nineteen elapses an edgy night
Thrusting into his books,
The story of motor bike,
Late night movie shows
Hakka noodles in a luxurious Chinese restaurant
Are like a myth for him.
Getting a sudden fragrance of jasmine
Is also beyond his thoughts.

The world before him
Is like a pristine canvas
Smooth and white-
No artist has ever tried his hand
In this virgin canvas.

10. A Wrong Road

This road is quite known to me
Even this T-junction too-
Is very much familiar ;
I frequented to this road many a time
I paused again and again
Reaching this T-junction
And got confused about which way to choose
Left or Right.

I cannot recollect
Which road I took the last time
Left hand side or right
Did I follow the same direction?
Did I go round the left time and time again?
Or it was always the right path that I followed.
And did the other roads
Remained unrevealed?
It would have been great
If someone picked up from before
Two separate videos
Of two different travelogues
Of these two roads.

It would be facile to juxtapose
The two roads of the left and the right
And judge the profit and the loss
I would not have misconstrued
Over and over again.

Or it would have been too tough
To choose the road
Through which I'd trod
One must have to pay back
For one's mistakes
Either on the left of on the right.

If I knew
On which ally of which road
The thorns of mistakes
Ambush clandestinely
Then I would have come to a stop
After reaching the T-junction,
And wayfaring would be stopped.

11. Living Like Mishti

Please come here, let me introduce you
With our Mishti
Mishti is the youngest member of our family.
You and I, we all need to learn to
Quite a great degree
From him.

Have you ever kept your eyes
Upon the wall mirror ?
Have you fixed your glance upon your eyes ?
Haven't you noticed the thicketed regret and repent
For the time
You have lost in the past ;
Along with that
A tremendous awe peeps through your eyes
That is the dread unknown
Thinking of the fluctuant tomorrow.

The two large eyes Mishti possesses
Are like a benign lagoon,
Greenish with the shadows of algae.
His tramping, his being alive–
And his every activity

Are only meant for today.

All he dislikes is
Raindrops, drizzles and shower
Yesterday was rainy,
For that reason
Mishti closed himself in a room
And spent the entire day put up with it
A suffering a great deal-
Though the day he left behind
Does not leave the faintest impression upon his mind

Rather he is enjoying thoroughly
The dazzling and sunny day today
He feels a wave of delight from within
And avail himself of it.
Mishti does not care about tomorrow
No fear he tames in his mind
Brooding about what will happen subsequently.

Eating his fill in three turns,
Strolling idly about in the neighbourhood twice a day
And a profound repose
Undisturbed, carefree and fully stretched out.
He never brings to his heel and never rue.
Only living on and on
For the day today.

Have you on earth
Thought of living like Mishti ?
Can you at all ?
Mishti is too endearing,
Too special to our family -
He is like the youngest son ;
To others
He may merely be a cat
But I can take an oath to tell that
You and I
The entire human race
Who are dissipated, wretched and astray,
Have lots of things to learn
From Mishti.

12. Will

Everything has to be set in due order
Every single trivial desire and every single reservations
Framing them one after another
A pyramid of desire has to be created.

It is a must to routinely water and fertilizer to
The lemon tree that Ma planted
In our kitchen garden.
This lemon tree gets rejuvenated every year
Even after being morbid and macabre.
Then its branches stoop with the burden of its fruits
And platoons of lemons roll about
Upon the floor of the bower.

It is mandatory to take great care
Of the Collection of Stories
Written by Sharat Chandra
In those estranged and scorched summer afternoons
Reading of Ramer Sumati
Being seated at the attic
Coagulated a heavy steam within the throat
And treasuring the extremely adorable memory
With the chest of our heart.

The most precious
And the ritziest gadget of our home -
The music system,
This was bought on debt.
Two mammoth speakers accompanied it as well.
Baba squared the accounts
Paying little by little every month.
The HMV records of Manna - Shyamal - Hemanta
Also have to be taken great care of.
And that bicycle-
Was the only companion and confidante
Of the fidgety grappling lad
After coming to the town
From his tiny hamlet.
Mounting upon his mute chum
He covered long distances
From Bolpur to Jamboni
And crossing Jamboni reached Prantik.
Numerous small but significant incidents
Which he experienced during his journey,
Of all those happenings,
The bi-cycle remained the lone and silent witness.

Making a will is none other than a necessity
Everything ought to be written respectively
Which enumerated articles

Have to be kept with great care.

Let the other things be dispensed among whoever you like

I have no objection to that.

13. Unbridled Words

Without any rehearsal
Creating no enigma, puzzle or riddle
Words simple, lucid and intelligible
With no metaphor added to them,
Are treasured within the chest.
They collide violently again and again
With the unblinking eagle-eyes
And breathe their last.

Consulting the dictionary
Choosing the words with vigil surveillance
Writing and tearing the script
Over and over again,
Exiling the mind
In a distant and unknown island,
They enmesh you rigorously
In the spider-web.

In this battle
All alluring stratagems, tricks and manueuvre
Are condoned.
No one harks back to a loser
And so there is no blood stain

In the trophy given to the champion.

In the no man's island
The exiled mind waits anxious, fretfully
Like a grumpy horse, it abrades its feet in the soil
For uttering the words treasured within the chest
And wait for the beckoning for the eyes
To get unbridled.

14. Recurrence

Vying continuously with the time
I have squandered away a lot of time.
To look back perpetually,
Turning my neck back over and over again
I have lost sight of a great many pictures.
Spread over the two sides of the road.
So, despite crossing long distance too
I frequently look back
To see the unseen pictures
Anew from the beginning.

I have broken myself many a time
To surpass and
To outdo my own self ;
I could see in me
The artist with his gluey mudded hands
Folded before his creator.
The artist
Amongst the scattered earthen arms, face
And broken heart
Sitting upon the patio of the cottage
At the place called Kumartuli.

The pile of my inaccuracies
Which often prick me
At the midnight
Like the cactus of deserts;
I take oath to myself
Again and again,
So that I never commit
The same inaccuracies
Any more time
By errors and omissions.
I am an amnesiac
Lose my mind time and again
With the curse of Durvasa, the wrathful sage.
Repeatedly I recompense
For my misgivings,
And a new cactus with its stabbing thorns
Is born again in the dessert.

15. The Merry-Go-Round

From Ahmadpur to Bolpur
From Sainthia to Lavpur
I sauntered about every fair
And spun round and round ;
Now on the horse back
And again mounted an elephant
Went up and down
On a slowly jerking motion.

In a fraction of a moment
Keeping my eyes tightly shut
I reached beyond the seven perilous seas and seven rivers,
Where live the telltale birds-
Bangoma and Bangomi.

The comb of amorous breeze
Raked my head of hair
And murmured in my two ears
The stories of Arabian Nights
And the distant strains of its melody
Resonated in my ears.

As I opened my eyes

A familiar world embraced
As I stretched my hands
There were Baba and Ma
Who provided me with a shelter
Of faith, dependence and affection.
Smile on their face
Lit up the dark.

I hardly have any idea
When and how
My little world of the merry-go-round
Had an abrupt change–
Now I am on board a roller coaster.
Clasped tight
The railings of the two sides of my cage
Sound of air
Like two arrows
Is passing through the sides of my ears
My entire body
Running in a serpentine motion
From the hades to more profound hades.

Eyes cannot be shut
My inflictions get puffed up
And crowd upon my two eyelids;
I have no leisure
To stop or to brood

Or to convey my views.

I am the lone commuter
Of the roller coaster
Day after day
Every day
I am increasingly being estranged
From my own
World of the merry-go-round.

16. Today, Tomorrow And Beyond

Forty years have elapsed
Within a blink of an eye
It is only today
That is here and now forever.

Today's cold
How piercing and frigid cold it is !
Along with it, the pattering of continuous rainfall
Accompanied by the icy wind
Makes the body and the mind
More and more doleful and melancholy.

But do you remember that winter?
Which was the place - Bhutan or in Sikkim
Within the chilly cold
We all assembled by the fireplace
There was tremendous thunder storm outside;
The memory of that wintry night
Knocks my mind over and over again.

Peradventure in some future day
I might be able to salvage

That chilly night again.
Probably would repossess
That pattering rainfall and chilly wind.

• 39 •

Today's day
Broods over some pensive strain
Filled with desperation and gloom.
It waits anxiously
When will the next day ensue?
But strangely, today's day
When becomes yesterday
It seems more endearing and appealing -
And it dazzles in the treasury of remembrance.
The present has little value
Being squeezed between the past and the future
So it ever strives to remain alive, being yesterday
Or perhaps it desires to dream
About the impending future.

17. Plain And Simple Life

Plain and simple
An Austere and home-spun life-
I implore you to
Wait for just a few days;
Devising has been on the go for long days together -
In the list of the long wrapping
There are the accounts
Of numerous thorough - going concoction;
A meticulous ticking is a must
In each and every box;
A small grey pencil
Would have been worth working
But there is a saying -
'Safe bind safe find',
So a sharp ivory knife
Is grappled within the bunch of five fingers.
It stabs at a venture
Upon the chest of
The crumbled yellowish paper,
Its lungs becomes perforated
In some places
Making it visible one end to other.

Plain and simple life -
But a lot of complicated sums
And quite a few riddles have to be solved
To be able to reach you !

A move cannot be made in the board of the Ludo
For the want of the yellow pawn
The infantry of the chess
Sit back stricken with languor
Thinking of a dashing stallion.
The end of the jigsaw puzzle
Is reluctant of being accomplished
Searching with thorough diligence too
Trace of the last stake of the puzzle
Is found.

I kept no paucity in putting efforts
Hundreds of red corpuscles
Of the artery, I freight
In the box of the yellow pawns of the Ludo,
The infantries move like horses
Mounting each other's back
And the last stake of the jigsaw puzzle
Is made
By cutting their bones.

All these arduous efforts

Certainly have some significance -
Because at the last of
All the efforts
A plain and simple life awaits •
An Austere and home - spun life.

18. The Predicament Of A Crazy Devotee of Cricket

Win or lose - both make a game
It was always there and will be in future times too.
You are though a professional player
Win or lose in a game
Is not a battle of survival for you.

Here I am
A crazy devotee of cricket
In my eyes too
The game is not at all
A battle of survival;
My predicament is that
The victory or defeat in this game
Is much much more than
The question of survival to me.

You lose a game
Your analyst
Makes you get up by rote
By mentioning when, where and why

You have erred,
A crowd of instructions, counsels and advice
Swarms up in your brain.

You try very hard
To put your mistakes to right
For winning in the next game;
But my predicament is that
For your petty errors and mistakes
I lose my appetite for a long day
And a weird pain wakes me from bed
In the middle of night suddenly.
Your mistakes unremittingly moves
Before my eyes, like a movie reel.

Does Chetan Sharma recollects,
His folly?
When he was milked a sixer
In the last ball of the match.
But Chetan's that non-performance
Still extensively open in my mind.
I feel the agony of a formidable nightmare
Until this day, for that down of his luck.

You being a professional cricketer,
Have the direct support
Of your personal trainer

And of your psychoanalyst;
That is the reason why
You roam about carefree and unperturbed
You listen to songs and chat happily
With a mind free from care
You prepare yourself at the same time
For winning in the next game.

But my predicament is that
When I lose
I feel myself completely alone
In the play-ground,
At that juncture,
I feel the entire world
To be my adversary.

Be that as it may
I continue living on
With the treasures in my mind -
A few precious moments.

That six successive sixers
Hit by our Yuvraj Singh
And that squandering of his t-shirt
Like the national flag of India
By Dada Sourav, in Lord's
Keep my mind as fresh as ever.

I get ready for the next game
Win or lose-both make a game
It is not a battle of survival
But much much more than that.

19. The Life Perhaps…

The door moves inaudible
Only to a single direction, like a clock
If it could be moved in the opposite way
Some errors may have been put to right.
Could get rid of
A great number of accidents
The life perhaps …

I'd have never missed
The local train of six in the evening
I would meet Sumana
Much ahead of time
Of the cutting of cake
The bouquet of flowers would not have dried up
In the palms
After waiting for so long
The life perhaps …

Waking up in the middle of night
At Ma's yoo - hoo
I would not have mistaken Baba's stomach pain
To be gastritis,
And would not have provided him with antacid

If I could know the pain to be the sign of heart attack
I would certainly call a cardiologist
The life perhaps …

Bhombal was standing at the roadside
He was waiting for none other than me -
He intimated me
That he said some urgent talk;
I was also in a hurry that day
I vowed to meet him on Saturday.
Bhombal did not talk to me any further
News came on that very night
My ill - fated friend Bhombal had taken parathion
And surrendered himself to death.
The thought ever pricks me now
If I would listen to Bhombal that day
Shutting my eyes to all work
The life perhaps …

The door moves gently and calm
Like a clock - to the same direction
Escapades renews our lives
And life's intercourse gets commuted.
How hard the endeavour may be
The door cannot be moved in the opposite direction
If we could succeed, the life perhaps …

20. Middle Class

Oh what a roar is heard from the veins
Like there are seeds inside the blood
Polishing is implied merely upon the canes
Mind with enclosed wall is stick-in-the-mud.

Handicap from the very birth
Vanquished from the start
All the sins would be out of hearth
In the germy water of the Ganges-gut.

Accustomed in parrot-fashion
Pig's-ear in discretion,
Denial to comply with elders' notion
Is not a rightful resolution.

Moving with circumspection
Considering omega and alpha if you say
Not to commit a single mistake
All the follies ought to pay.

Fondness fetches in enormous harm
No sin is severer than if you make love
Live on with a wooden heart, must not there be any charm

Agastya, the sage cursed this, and he still looks from 'bove.

This is not at all my mistake
Rahu lodged in our ancestors' fate,
Whenever you take a break
Your palm will go on to threat.
Middle class by birth they are
The term has become their middle name
Middle class are kept at par,
With the grace of a thousand problem.

21. This Very Consummation

So many varied colours
Stay touching the bust of the high
A small yellowish pied beauty
In the couple coloured sky purple
Deep red and light brown
You thought it to be
An artist's impression of sunset
But did not notice
The rainbow of the rising sun
In the mirror - like blobs of water
Reflecting upon the alabaster wings of birdies.

Trickles of water
Or it is the briny perspiration
Pledged for thousands of years
Of a wearied sailor.
It is the rainbow
Or red, white and green silts
In the veins,
As a piece of evidence
Of being alive.

Dying as a proof
Of being alive
Or keep on living
By dying every single day bit by bit;
Evidence of being alive
Or sanction for death
Nerves one by one capitulate
In the spider web
Of numerous complicated questions.

Sunset and the rising of the sun
Are the trick of a single colour
Mirrors of bloody sweat and the rainbow
Hold the palpitation of one and the same life
The difference is hardly there
Between dying and being alive
The very consummation of that moment Remains triumphant
at the last

22. An Earthen Lamp Within The Chest

Long time elapsed
Being the earthen lamp of the altar of Tulsi
The fire within my chest
Is decaying leisurely.

The falling leaves of the imminent winter
Get the fragrance of soil from nearby
Storm would come someday
And so, you and I are kept waiting.

I carefully arranged the snags and thorns
Keeping them with
I diffused the last hours of the night.
Narrating sagas and myth.

Few stayed and few deserted
Leaving slips of recollections
How could I stop them
How all bring to an end.
When the end begins
Does it come in stealth or with a roar
Then the sun and moon

Both get extinguished all of a sudden.

The tamarisk loses its foothold
Day by day
Let the ocean-like-sky decline
Let the evening lamp be lit
For a few days more
Within the chest case.

23. Amigo

You stand leaning against the wall
I cannot bear your pain,
Getting an amigo like you
Not an easy bounty to gain.

Your eyes are filled with tears
When you see the eyes in mine,
This is the mark of a true friend
With not a single tricky sign.

I have spent such a long span
Keeping my eyes up you,
I am changed that no way was told
Amenable time never changes its hue.

We meet every now and then
On no account you switch,
The third eye of the sightless king
Judhistir devoid of any hitch?

I fire arrows aiming at you
How many in unit they may be,
Crowd of love and emotion

All they get back to me.

You are peerless as an amigo
Such a friend do not wait in a row
You stand leaning against the wall
The mirror to portray all weal and woe.

24. The Dread

A long route has been crossed
In dread, covered it being surreptitious,
This dread has been reared within mind
Since I was born and became conscious.

Long since I feared of super naturals such as
Ghost, spectre, apparition, wraith and spook,
In the interplay of light and shade of the lantern
What creates masquerade on the earthen roof at the nook?

So many times I woke up from the bed in dread
Mumbled, muttered and talked under my breath,
The long sums of subtraction and addition
Brought me in close proximity to death.

As an exam put to an end
Another started knocking my door,
The storm of dread grew and grew
And made my pre-teens extremely bore.

I espied my maiden love where the tuition I took
She smiled like dew and moved as if she was a tender leaf,
Abani Sir caught me once and stared at me with such frown

I felt lonely for the first while and it filled my heart with grief.

I learnt to fear the sun of the autumn
And the untimely rain of the summer,
I dreaded almost all the seasons
And all life, I remained a mummer.

I always dreaded to miss a train
That leaves in the middle of night
Though I stood in the row from quite before
But never ceased to fear missing the train's flight.
Dread became my constant companion
I embraced my dread very tight,
Empty would be my life when I thought
Dread could ever disappear from my sight.

Today when I look back to my past
Realise what a fool I had been,
There would have been no peril
If I just had some courage to preen.

Amulets that rounded my neck and stones in my fingers
The galaxy of planets in the sky, created an angst in me
If I could throw off you all, send far away from my reach
Entire power play of dread will fade whatever there may be.

Surpassing all dread then at last

Leaving only one residue,
If I shall have enough time
To tell all-adieu-adieu !

• 59 •

25. So Near Yet So Distant

You are now much nearer to me
Mobile phone, ipad, Laptop
I reach you simply with a touch.

I see you on Facebook
Your latest Hollywood pix
Are selectively arrayed on it
Which country is that? Switzerland or Croatia?
I know you so intimately
And so, those unknown countries are also
Much known to me.

I do not need to wait
Nowadays
For your letters
The message box on WhatsApp
Are always filled with your messages
Scantly I erase them
For making some room.

On the contrary, all your letters
I still treasure indomitably

Within the wooden box, granny conferred to me.
I see so many of your followers
So many men's hashtag on Twitter
I see your roaming over the places
I see your thoughts
All are within my near proximity.

You are so near
Still, I have not listened to
Your voice for so many days
There was a time, when
I spent the entire day
Listening to your words.

Your pictures
Covering the social media
A smiling face
Transparency of neon light in the street;
Your eyes but reflect a crowd of
Weariness and gloom–
No one understands their meaning
Within the throngs of emojis.

You are now much nearer to me
Only scarcely I miss
Your voice
Your letters

Filled with whole and unbroken alphabets
And I profoundly miss
The springy warmth of your mellifluous derm.

26. At Last

I was also there that day
At the helm of the procession
My arms fisted in fury
Visage reflecting excitement
I gave my voice
To the mountain-cleft
Roar of the seas.

But not a tiny ripple
I noticed in your stone eyes
You were mute and aphonic.

A scattering crowd ordained
To reach you
Holding my head high
With great pride
Cutting across the carcasses;
I obeyed their order
Word for word and verbatim.

But when I arrived
At your patio
I found your room vacant

You were not there.

I clasped fire
Within my bunch of five
I wove a net with all my cardinal passions
So that efficacies of the foes can be trapped.

As near as I reach
I increased dart-velocity,
Though I became distant
And more distant from you.
At last leaving me behind alone
My foes got back
To their homes
Tomorrow's pride
Has taken the form of ash
And lying on the floor.

My spine leaning
Is drooped deep
Between the two knees;
At this moment
I hear the sound of your footstep
When I hush all the other sounds.
When I am a wearier vanquished in thousands of battle
I feel the touch of your lips
Upon my forehead.

In your stone-eyes, percolating with affection
I took note of an applause for a triumphant!

27. Selfie

Grey mirror could not hold
The river bed in low tide,
I failed to realize why I am a mote
To all and why they keep me aside.

The reason first was detected
When I met myself in a camera phone,
Among the crowd of millions of faces
Pulls me back the lone face of my own.

What an inordinate creation is it !
I am thoroughly stricken with its marvel;
If the Mother Nature inspected into it
Would have withdrawn it into her own cell.

The mountain of these loads of photos
Hard drive go wrong to harbour,
Hence I delete them all those files
I am nowhere to be found, not in a single picture.

It has become the fashion of my eyes
I chuckle now and then seeing myself in that guise
How much I see I desire for more

I fall deep in love with myself, it has become a happy lore.

It reminds me of the Prince Narcissus
Who spent hours watching himself in the river water,
The world has fallen in an abrupt cessation
Only the jealousy of love is lit in strong ardour.

Standing and dangling at the bank of the river
Like the flower of Daffodil,
So precious is each and every second
Lest me, does anybody feel?
The sole disgrace is that
This I, will never come in for me
He will ever remain as a selfie
Suicidal deception will go on to pree.

28. Friend

We could see each other
In Facebook leaves in glee,
And in the library of WhatsApp
My friend if you be.

Being a friend is pretty easy
Though there are some conditions,
Friends remain alive
In selfie taken from camera phones.

I heard that long ago
One can be most fortunate,
Finding a pink bordered sky blue sharee
Among a library of books to ornate.
In a cubicle crammed with books
Time came to a sudden pour leur,
When touch of fingers could nudge
The chest of the Baul warbler.

It is really strange, in those days
Having a solo friend clinched a lot,
We elapsed together the entire day
It was equally ours whatever we sought.

But now it all changed
Today's affairs if you see, are different, in every way
A hundred and ten friends encircling me
Now sway and then get away.

If you enable I make you my friend
Engaging no effort or wuv-
Go when you wish to go
'Cause it engages no oath or no love.
Take fancy to serf my page
Whenever you come online,
Press 'like' button in all my posts, no matter you like it
Or not, just a click, will make me fine.
Not many days I posted my photo
Standing by a rose tree
Wise friends all ascertained
My necklace had been so worthy.

Or that day when I went to a programme
Among a large and clinching crowd,
Whose house what that I can't remember
About what? I have doubt.

What does it matter, who or what
The focal symbol is myself was there,
Selecting from the hundreds of clicks

I posted some nice ones and clear.

If you be my friend
I could share with you,
Variety of sharees, makeups
And precious stones of different hue.

It seems you brood a lot
What's there to think so much?
Don't be pensive in that extent,
Small world here free for all
Within the yashmak of amity-consent.

So at last from today
We have become friends with each other.
Keep it in mind that my world
Moves round 'like' button which is though uther.

29. In Search Of A Dream

I need a dream
Like a short story, closely knit,
And must be fraught with suspense
From the beginning up to the feet.

The visages of the dramatis personae
Ought not be vague but incandescent and immaculate;
There should not be any murk or haze
In their demeanour and movement-
They are to be men of flesh as in reality.

From one scene to other
They must move unpremeditatedly,
Without losing the clue of dialogues ;
There should be no fear of breaking my slumber
And no terror of losing the memory of the dream
And consigning them all to oblivion
It is painful failing to lose sight of the dream
After one is awake.

I have no role to play in this dream
Am merely a spectator of it–

It is like, I have bought all the tickets
Of a movie hall
And only my presence is felt
I am here see the grandeur at its height.

I wish even after I wake from my sleep,
The dream would not pass from my sight,
In the dazzling day light.
Each and every scene and dialogue
Must be treasured in my mind as it is,
And the shadow of the dream
Move to and fro clinging to my-self.

My slumbers lost their colour
For the want of dreams
There is neither any charm left in sleeping anymore
Nor excitement attached to it;
Not the scarcity of sleep but the dream
I lack,
The dream, which must be fraught with suspense
Like a telefilm, that would hold close to my sleep
And weave in it the desire of seeing new dreams
Throughout the night.

30. Our God

He lies silently
At the portico of the temple
His entire body daubed with dust
After making a long journey;
Cool touch of marble of the portico
Gives him peace of mind
This comfort is nothing but
The God's solace to him.

The stony deity
Is merely an idol to the temple-priest
Variety of troublesome thoughts pry into his mind
Amid the eye-pestering fumes of joysticks
And blackening light of the earthen lamp.

He worries about the expenses of education
Of his youngest son,
Wedding of his daughter
And the decaying and declining health
Of his wife-
He calculates in his mind
That priesthood will not work for long
He needs to seek refuge of some other god

Somewhere else.

A heap of steaming rice
Piled upon the sal-leaves
Resembling to a small mountain.
The labourer of brick kiln
Takes a long breath
Keeping his eyes close.
He is happy with the thoughts of home-coming
And his face gleams with complacency.
He takes a deep breath and feels the aroma of warm rice
God's balmy body perhaps smell alike!

The boy-chick, a tiny angel,
Cannot recollect his mother's face even a bit,
She left him, when he was one and half year of age
The little mother had succumbed to an acute anemia.

His mother comes to his dreams
And he imagines her wearing a sharee
Having a broad lengthwise furbelow in the border
And she having a large fingertip of vermilion
Sparkling upon her forehead
How can this face be different from God?

The ungovernable romping lad, very tiny though
Running around inside and outside home

Getting over through dodging,
Rise up immediately if fallen
And plunge into his mom's lap.
He giggles with joy and
Few of his little milk teeth
Like Shiuli flowers are revealed–
His mom's heart shores high with rapture
And she sees God's smile in her sons face.

In the silent corridors of the hospitals
In the smothering crowd of the casualty
In the delivery suit
Or in the bellows of the ventilator
Prayers of numberless people
Ebb and flow–
Aiming at one and the same God.

31. I Shall Be Depraved Now

Giving a coupe de glow
To my delicacy in doing unseemly,
I shall unmask my sociability,
And repealing my fourteen forefathers

Staying in the cage
My Baul Warbler is choked
During the last days of her life,
A mountain of deceit is accumulated with
I shall repay all my debt
And let all my love be unleashed
I shall be depraved now.

Tucking my bed with the thorn of Mansa
I have estranged from the flowers,
Who desires to live depraved
Gets rid of all the confines of mind,
For loving to a greater extent
I shall be depraved now.

For enjoy adulterous lust
And to observe it from a different angle,

I shan't choose a simple man
But he must be complex and crooked,
I shall love to lead Draupadi's life
And shall be depraved now.

To give leniency to your wish
I shall be depraved now,
To burn you in the fire of envy
I shall be depraved now.
To come close more closer,
I shall be depraved now.
To make my soft spot more soft
I shall be depraved now.

32. Friend's Wife

I fancied you much much later
And had met my friend long before.
The day I saw you is so vivid in my mind
That it seems to be the saga written offshore.

I got the drift of you so close
That I can still remember the Sharee you wore that day
The colour of that is still green in my mind
In which arm did you tie the Titan watch, a notice I pay.
How did you style you hair-in bun or in braid
How some locks you fair face hey lay !

I liked you demeanour at the first look
The way you chortled like a highlander cascade
Open and fresh, in your two profound and greeny eyes
I saw a stoical strangeness as of a Baul Warbler amid masquerade.

Mention of my friend is needless here
Both we were born in same neighbourhood.
Same year to born probably we share
Inseparably united from heart, all know, from childhood.
My friend is a bit circumspect

Perhaps a bit pensive and a little capricious
But to me he is larger than life in matter of getting claps
From other, he is not at all covetous.
Although we are friends inseparable by heart
But we are very much distinguished at a point
In one place we are just opposite
As black and white, if God us to anoint.

My friend has never made a bit of time
To see the cascade of a mountain and how it fall
Never was he under the impression of
Why the green put an indifferent to lull.

He could not lend some time to see
The dialect of two forest-bound eyes,
Every lore carries with it in its climax
A wordless and devil-may-care cries.

These yearnings has no future and so
The dialect of love blinkers like the glow-worm,
Tiny and timid that fire of envy
Plunges into the water of cascade in swarm.

My friend and I both have
A great fortune of amity,
Rocky cascade gets the form of a mirage so close
Yet much distant owing to our rationality.

33. An Eternal Appendage

You were there from the very first day
Adhered with me thoroughly through and through
But I was unable to recognize the fact.

I was surrounded with
An ocean of darkness
How glibly drowned and floated
I thought perhaps I am alone
Yet you were always with me.

Suddenly one day
The ocean water receded away
And the touch of harsh wind
Cuffed my entire body.
I was repelled from the spacious comfy of dark
And in no time exposed to the blazing light of thousand lamps

I was terrified to feel myself in that dazzling world of light
And at that very moment
I felt your existence.

That was the beginning-

Gradually I perceived
The magnitude of this inseparable extant
Between you and me.

I have nothing that could be hidden
To you,
That of my mischievous childhood
And that warp and woof of my adolescence.
Or the intricate paradox of my middle age.
You are the lone and silent spectator
Of all these episodes of adventures.

My own cognates
And the friends who were nearest to my heart
Left me forlorn one after another;
Some of them left me directed by their will
And some got compelled with profound reluctance,
But my attachment with you
Remained as fresh as the day I breathed my first.

I rest assured and repose peacefully
Cause I know you are ever in surveillance,
By my side until I exist in this globe.
The rise and fall of this complicated machine,
Acute and intense mystery of each and every cell,
The entire affair of this system is at your finger-tips.

We go on with our amity the same way
Maintaining time's fixated rhythm
We commute, transpose and transform
The harsh wide curls up both our corium.
We two become blind concomitantly
Being exposed to the blazing light of thousand lamps

We both close our eyes
Simultaneously wait for that dark ocean;
Both we dream of plunging into the water deep
And inhaling our chest full
You and I–
Bound in an eternal appendage.

34. A Fairy Tale

The entire night tomorrow
Under the flood light
I have played football,
What a great control I had
Upon the ball !
Just like Maradona or Messi
I dribbled through the defenders
One after another
And gently placed the ball
Over the goal keeper's head
And wrapped it
In the net of the goal post.

I took a free kick
Like David Beckham,
The ball struck to the corner of the goal post
And got back.
It was a narrow escape
For the goal keeper of the opponent team.

And I got a chance taking a penalty shot
At the stoppage time,
I had held the ball close to my chest,

Removed the weltering dusts and sands
From its surface, with great affection
And then I placed it upon the grass.
Then keeping the eyes
Straight upon the eyes of the goal keeper,
Pushed the ball towards the remotest corner
Of the goal post at the right hand side
And it was a goal!
The poor goalkeeper plunged aiming at the left side.

All the above incidents happened last night
Within my dreams-
In reality
Playing Football is beyond my capacity
I cannot even walk-
My legs had become paralysed
Owing to an accident,
I am completely dependent
And rely only upon my wheelchair.

Yesterday night, after many an ages
I cuddled, nuzzled and caressed you deep–
Even after elapsing so many harsh seasons
The hide of your body
Is still so pappy and soft, so plain-
Like the back of that milk-white swan
Which I left in the distant and forlorn island !

Your bare back smells of the tamarisk
That was known to me so close,
Inarticulate sagas of love and languishment
Brimming over from each and every follicle
Kept me over-ornate all night long.

Unending stories did not end
And my dream met with a break
With the sound of calling bell,
It was the time of the arrival of my cleaner.
Long since I have not beheld you visage
Your voice had been inaudible to me for long too,
Yet I loved you too intense
Last night in my dreams.

The desires which will never be fulfilled–
The incidents which had been drifted into oblivion,
Are protected and treasured with great care
Under the superintendence of some movie reels;
They appear before our unwinking eyes
One after another
Detecting appropriate time and state
And measuring our type and trait
Then pans out slowly
Some incredible fairy tales-
Ceaselessly, in the dreams

35. Autobiography Of A Flowering Cherry

You resemble a lot to your grandpa
There is no conifer as old as mine in this bower
I beheld your grandpa
From the time he was of your age.
He used to caress my veined, arid and prickly skin
With his tiny and soft hands,
Just as you do at the present time.

Your grandpa climbed up the oscillator
Suspended with a coconut string
From my right arm,
He moved back and forth sitting on it
As he got back from school.

Whatever thoughts and talks accumulated
Being the steams of words within his heart
Throughout the day in school,
He went on murmuring incessantly, sitting near me.
Perhaps he felt sort of a relief
When the words he fetched out
As an unshackled cascade unleash itself
Splitting the breast of a mountain.

Your grandpa, almost a bundle of joy to me
Continued his monologue sitting patiently
He ceaselessly depicted incidents after incidents
And annexed words after words in his oration.
My sole responsibility was to listen to him
Silently and without saying a word.

Coming and going of the seasons
Entangled your grandpa's entire mind and soul
Throughout the year.

When the chilly cold weather attacked me in the winter
Your grandpa invigorated, stimulated and cheered me,
And together we twiddled our thumbs
For the delightful month of Phalgun.

Then suddenly one day
A few tiny Cherry buds gigged their faces
Drawing out the snow of my body !
How much these Cherry buds took
The breath of your grandpa away,
Really I cannot express in words.
His eyes and face teemed with joy,
He embraced me with his two little hands
And whispered in my ears-
'Basanta Ese Gechhe'

(The Spring Has Arrived).

Years after years
Seasons after Seasons
Your grandpa and I elapsed together,
I witnessed your grandpa aging gently
The complexion of his body transformed
From a resplendent and sparkling green to
A cordial and cooling yellow of the season of Hemanta–
The hue of your grandpa's skin
Reminded me of the colour of the attire
Generally put on by the Bauls,
Stoical persons they are, apathetic to worldly interests.

Years passed by and in the last winter,
I was scarcely able to chance your grandpa,
He used to wave his hand ever and anon
From the window of a room,
His bedroom was at the first floor.
I felt a strange kinship with your grandpa
When I saw, my arms and most of their branches
Resembled his arms,
Arid, veined and weak were they, as I now possess.
One day again
A few tiny Cherry buds gigged their faces
Drawing out the snow of my body !
And that very day I chanced not your grandpa

But a smile of Cherry buds
In your milky white milk teeth,
And it gave me a feeling that,
The very smile can bring you near to me !

Now you keep your two hands tiny and soft
Upon my drowsy and wearied body
And whisper in my ears–
How much elated it is for me to listen to
Your grandpa's word from your mouth–
Heartening with hope and promise–
'Basanta Ese Gechhe'
(The Spring Has Arrived).

36. An Ode To the King

Five or six seasons I see the world
An alien camp keeps me in
With my Ma
My nine brothers and sis,
Baba's memory is somewhat blurred
My nine brethren, sis and I
Grew for a few days within a single tent
Under this alien camp.

I'm grateful to you my King !
I've not been brought up in a refugee camp.

They said,
Only an ocean in front
Somehow to cross to reach the dreamland,
I went through many a seas
And now darkness and I are imprisoned
In a scant quarter of a frowsy basement.

Some wizard hyenas approach
Like a scary nightmare
They have sharp nails
Smelling like dried blood and sweat.

They gradually tweak the girl
Snatching the seeds of her dreams.

Though I stand still
Under the ocean blue sky
My dreams do not get entangled in the snare of the hyenas
O King, I'm so,
Too grateful to you.

Her wild eyes
Are sheathed with a strip of dark blackness
No light can enter them,
They are encircled with gaged
Silence of the world.
Her feet are languid, unconscious
A wheelchair captivates her acquiesce.

But I run through the world
From one end to another.
Emancipated independent am I,
I see the seasons come and go
With changing colours.
My mind rejuvenated with
Sounds of falling rain, bird's fluttering wings!

O my King-

As I'm so easy going, so normal and so general
As I roam, as I breathe
Paint and dream
Staying at a small mundane nook.

Your kindness
Makes all these possible
I'm grateful so
Indebted to you forever !

37. Faces Of Agony

Your face floats in sixty inch television
In latest colour pixel and in high definition
Lines of your face are so clearly visible ;
Your face
From all over the world floats
Within my living room
Various faces from
Various nations, various races.
It's like a procession of faces of agony.

Faces of six month old innocence
Faces of ancient hapless ones
All keeps their presence felt in my habitat.

I know not their language
And it's not needed too
As no face has words.
Faces of agony are distorted
A lump of flesh
Like a broken mirror.

Face of a mother
Turns and twists on my television

From Sichuan
Corpse of her thirteen year old daughter
Under the dungeon is found
Of a school collapsed in an earthquake.

Again mudded face of a father from the city of Mariupol
Comes to my vision (tele)
He gets back burring his only son,
Whose chest had been furrowed in a gun shot.

Ajmal Ali from Noyakhali
Stands still at the shore of
The flow tide of the Padma
He lost his parents here once
In a boat wreck.

A baby of six months
In the orphanage of Basra
Not at all thinks of his future
All his face of agony shows
Is thirst for a morsel of food !

There goes on
A procession of thousand empty faces
On the screen of my luxuriant television
These faces turn and twist every now and then
But the screen is completely indifferent

To all these faces of agony
Signs of distortion fails to touch it and
Hence the LCD screen of my newly fangled television
Ever remains flawless with not even a sign of wrinkle!

38. Compensation For Aberration

Quite a few years
He elapsed
Without doing any aberration,
It would be wrong to tell that he didn't do any aberration
Rather it's better to say,
It did not seem to be an aberration
To his friends and neighbours
What he used to do.

As he would come out
With his trumpet & cymbals
At the crack of dawn in autumn
For the invocation of Durga, the mother Goddess.
He would sing Agomoni songs
And the entire neighbourhood used to awake to it.

In the monsoon
When river touched patio of each house
The man transformed the vessels meant for putting fodder
To the buffaloes into a small canoe
And float himself in water,
He would create a mountain

Of the floating mangoes from the orchard
Within his watercraft and distributed them in each house Of
the neighbourhood.

In chilly wintry nights
He sought the lost calf
And brought it to its mother cow
With the help of merely a lantern.

With the passing of time, there was an abrupt change
Rooms became bright with colour televisions
People now watch TV series waking all nights
Dawns started to be spent in snoring and sleeping deep
Neighbours got irritated with any obstacle to it.

The mango orchard was mown
And replaced with series of cottages
The stormy river slowly perished
With the notoriety of the city dwellers, who started living in
them.

The man who never did any aberration
Sold all his belongings
Lands, farms, cattle and many more And came to the city to
build his nest In an apartment of two rooms. Thus began the
factum of his aberration, One after another.

Heap of these aberrations Gradually subdued a frank and candid A complete folksy life.

Know not, which way
To look for comfort
But the future generation
Could never meet up
The compensation of this aberration.

39. Story Of My Ma And A Cave

My Ma lately tells
Of a cave, many a time
The light in the cave lies dead
Though no door covers its way.
My Ma calmly stands in front of the cave
She pines
To enter it,
But fails to do so
Though no door covers its way.

If she could
She could reminisce perhaps
Of a naïve lass of seventeen
Who had left city and came crossing the river Kopai
To enter a holy wedlock,
With the mentor of a tiny burg.

Perhaps she could recollect
That princely lad,
Village folks looked upon whom as outlandish.
In reality, this man was a genuine artist.
Once he went to study medicine in Kolkata.

In an Anatomy class,
He denied to dissect corpses
And found his way back to his ancestral home in the village.

The lad stood unfaltering and believed that
Though mortals die
Their inner dreams
Remain fresh and keep living on.

Like the cave
The inner part of Ma's brain
Is also filled with blackness
Else she could recollect
The days of dire poverty-arid and burnt
In the air of the month of Chaitra.

Her husband was a genuine artist and poet
Honesty built his frame.
He uttered with pride-
We may be penny less but not derelict of values.
Hence Ma draped rugged sharees
Hunger persisted in utensils
As she fed her three siblings.
Ma halts in front of the cave
She cannot recollect
Of her worship
In Phullora temple of Lavpur,

Of the mango tree at the yard of our rented house
At Amodpur
Ma even cannot reminisce her heaving a sigh of relief
At her own house at Bolpur
That she acquired selling all her jewelry.

Life stories are paired one after another
Within the black cave
Just like the reels of a movie,
But the lamps of the projector
Cannot be lit anymore,
Hence the path of both mind and eyes
Remains occluded
With the murk of the cave
Though no door covers its way.

40. In Anatomy Class

At last the man
Looked upon himself to be in luck,
So long his nights were spent in bypath
Tucking rugs upon dust and bristly rocks
And now he is lying straight
On a long megalith
Of stone alabaster.

He hasn't bathed well for long
And longed to dip in the Ganga
But his wish could not be meet up.
Here his entire body is sanctified with antiseptic shower,
The room fills with pungent smell of formalin.

Lying straight on the long megalith
Of stone alabaster,
The man thinks of the coming days.
He'll be sent for anatomical test tomorrow,
Test will be circumstantial
From toe to brain

He had never put on shoes
Soles of his feet

Are too hard so.
The doctors will face trouble
To pierce this rhino-hide !

Left leg is shorter
He had a narrow escape that night
Run over
By a sports car of a boozehound,
When he was in slumber.

Inside the stomach
The body carries an ulcer.
And lungs take the load of
Congealed dust, dart, smoke
And smudge of carbon.

Only his heart within four walls
Is carefully kept without any burden,
It craves not to vanquish
And all its arteries long to be alive.

But the man is concerned the most
About the nerves of his brain.
Would the researchers diagnose
That he was actually suffering from
An imposter syndrome ?
And he dreamt of being a star one day

Lying in a torn coverlet.

41. Banyan Tree

From far away, birds arrive
Like pieces of chewed strings-
They come to the banyan tree
To heal their maim wings.

Taking along her seven years nestling
His granny reaches the banyan,
Father left his Ma for another,
And the mother bereft
Dived down from seventh floor.
Granny leaves him
With the banyan
She is now appeased-
The kid
Is now undertaken by the banyan.

An elderly lady of seventy five
Had a name in culinary
Now knees kiss her back.
Unable to pair with son's ménage
She makes home under the banyan.

Is Shephali, a tenderly mother of three baby dolls,

Her husband banished her
For not yielding a son.
Deprived and dishonoured
She's sought refuge under the banyan tree.

Such various birds
Old, young, white, black or yellow
Find their nest in this banyan tree.
So many variety of birds stay in here
But all their breasts are gash and aggrieved
With the affliction caused by kith and kin
Deep these gushes
Takes, months, years and often a life
To recuperate.
Banyan beholds them
With its two protective arms
From which secrete cure
For all woes.

42. The Human Herbage

Herbage loses heart for want of human
Every here and there, it seeks for plenteous soil
Else saplings wouldn't see the sun
Cracked barks moan though none can see its toil.

Seasons' cadavers stay in the sand coffin
Sunburnt lips extend in vain
Shadow of death vale over the tree arms
Stealthily lengthen.

Olden memories vaguely appear
Rooted deep in mind
When a wayfarer's led astray by a simoom and reposes
They leave impression even after the man wakes.

Seawater washes decayed stone monuments
Human feat, dejection and pride assimilated
Ceases to exist on earth.

Plants due for want of human
Human perishes for want of plants
Plants slowly grow
Deep inside human

Destined to join hand in hand.

43. Melodrama

Few arrows left in my quiver
Have lost their acuity being used for numberless counts
Action same with new alter
Bluntness made them heft.

Many a man, not much before
Made a show of love, those saints adore,
From far and near
Reached to attain love at your door.

All these combatants returned vanquished
Inefficacious to hold their heads high
It was a mystery, that in me you saw that fire
And the arrow of my quiver impelled your heart.

My mind beamed hot, being boastful I thought
All my worries have gone,
Your last resort will become
The slave of the same arrow
My kisses will warm your fertile bed.

It's truly a pity that the same me and you
Couldn't remain like before

My arrows rust can't reach your heart
My touch lost that magic-words extraneous
Dumb commune causes speechless moan.

After brooding for long hours, finally I found a measure
The arrow that once impelled your heart
Rust that arrow as the last tool will
My crimp and undaunted arms maneuver
They'll pierce your heart in mine
And I remain victorious and this will be viable forever.
(Prosaic friends excuse me for this melodrama.)

44. A Plant Inside My Chest

Doctor says
A plant has taken its birth inside my mundane frame
Time unknown involuntarily
A seed of some fruit
Stealthily took refuge within my lung
Now with time and space
It has grown with all its stems beyond measure.

Crossing the lung
They have reached the four chambers of my heart.
Soon they will fling the doors open
And would emerge in the arteries red and blue
Like serpentine streams.

It's not possible anymore to lacerate the plant
Hence it needs to be dwindled by medication.
Dietician caused me learning by heart
Names of the food the plant relishes
I was strictly forbidden to have those.
Physiotherapist gave a long lecture
On the utility of some specified workout.

I though roam about here and there at ease
With a plant in my chest
Nobody knows of its existence inside me.

I destroyed all panacea, which would cause harm
To my plant
Its appetite matches mine
And now I love to have the food which it likes.

I long for that day
When the plant would explode shattering my chest
Once again my plant and I
Would breathe anew filling our chest!

45. Human Disease

I've been confined in this laboratory for the last ten days
All my cells, their molecules and atoms
Have gone through severe tests
By the researchers during the entire spell.

They measured the quantity of oxygen
In each of the red corpuscle in my blood
They gauged the wave of emotion in all the chambers of
my heart
About the rise and fall of the mercury
Curious they felt testing them in electroencephalogram.
Numberless statistics of each and every moment
Of these ten days are stored
In the hard-drive of the ultra-modern robot
They analyzed my future and past
With the help of graphs and charts,
Of different kinds red and blue
It would help the juvenile folks to get their PhD.

All were grave, in the disciplinary meeting, at last
Their opinion did not fall apart
They came under the same umbrella to find
There is no existence of my disease but of my mind.

I did not dare to tell them all
The disease took birth
From a different satellite
Once we knew it to be the earth.

I did not tell them
As they would have imprisoned me
In the cell for insane so.

46. Chitrangada

I am yet not prepared
You are also not matured entirely
We need a few more days
Before we remove all masks from our faces.

The mark of wound in my left cheek
Which has dried up with passing of time
Is still unknown to you.
Acid touched my face once
And the blemish of my lower chin
The burnt inertia of the skin
Does not become visible still in your horrible dreams.

Silent procession of countless masks
In the rows in grooves of wall
Regains life in conducive space;
Actors of theatres or folk plays
Continue to spell dialogues without knowing them
But memorizing all, like a parrot.

Face unseen behind the mask
Eyes remain unclosed though
Do they flummox and perplex ?

Do they show delinquent path
That leads to hellish trench?
And the sopping humane voice
Fills your eyes with tears.

Your eyes moist and wobbly feet
Lead you towards the hellish trench
Your infallible exile meets a blockade
When I hold your hands with all my might.

Hence both you and I
Find a nest
Cue of sleepless eyes
Voice in shifting oscillation like waves of the seas
And a balmy green touch
Of warm hands
Let they meet the want of the mask without face.

47. Lineage of A Sequoia

All goes well
Everything moves keeping the rules intact
The plant well grows but with passing phases
Green foliage beautify the sapling,
And fruits gradually appear from flowers
It when explodes the lives of seeds spread nearby
They establish their roots
Bending the mother plant
Dynasty of sequoia begins.

Still some seeds devil-may-care,
Who cannot be indoctrinated,
Come out tearing all the root stocks.
Typhoon become their friend
And they fly away upon the wings of temerity.

Far far away
Crossing seven perilous seas
They built their castle
In region unseen and unknown
Where horizon touches the soil.

Then again starts

The discipline of the known regime -
Green leaves beautify the new sapling
And fruits gradually appear from flowers.
Bending the mother plant
A new dynasty of sequoia begins.

Perhaps one day
Inquisitive eyes of a gypsy brat
Would scrutinize
The peculiar resemblance of the two dynasties
Which have grown thousand miles away from each other.

The king of the dynasty
The sequoia, who left home long ago
Tells the sprouts of his seed
The saga of the life he left behind.

Perhaps perhaps
Perhaps some day
One of those sprouts
Get back to the roots of the ancient sequoia
He would come out tearing all his present root stocks.
Perhaps he would embrace both the roots
And build a tenet
Which will be the bridge of the lost lineage.

48. Sorrow Of the Verse

•

Don't be aggrieved my Verse
Nobody lest I
Understands your grief;
Being grievous is none other than your being in a state of
splendour
As the rainbow all over the sky
When thunder storm ceases to be.

Or it's like the water upon lotus leaves
A precarious moment caught in
The mirror of pearl-water.

Time is too tough nowadays
Adding word to word
Breast ripping inarticulate wailing cry
Like the dogs of pathway
In full moon night.

So your grief and you
Cling each other
At the leaves of issues which come during the pujas
Fog of emotion like steam
Get congealed

At the corner of the eyes.
In the procession of umpteen people
Deaf and dumb
Various pathos
Deposit at the nook of the pair of their eyes.
Reflection of blood, sweat
And crudest reality.

Being grievous is none other than your being in a state of
splendour
If compared with their anguish
So it's not time
To appreciate your grief.

Both you and I wait for the moment
When the sad commoner again
Be emancipated from their anguish
By drenching in your grief.

49. The Word Unspoken

An indomitable desire to see her once
Goes driving me on
Though it's not much required;
Perhaps meet not her is preferred
In a simple immaculate middle class household.
It would be like bringing a storm for no cause.

The desire is not like
To swoop into the fire
Or audacious journey to the ocean full of jaws
For bringing pearls,
Or expedition to the Everest
Without oxygen.

The desire is quite like setting bare feet
On the grass, wet with dew
In the dawn of autumn -
Or it's like listening with eyes closed
To the buzzing of jingles
After crossing uproars of the outer world.
Or the smell of comfort
Coming out of the dry soil
After a shower of rain.

Seeing her once is pressing
'Cause a word unspoken
Waits patiently among the crowd of words
It longs to touch the fire
Like a butterfly -
What remain unfulfilled are
The touch of the grass wet with dew
Buzzing of the jingles
And the smell of comfort
Coming out of the dry soil.

50. The Album Of Black And White Photos

Among a box full of
So many marbles of various colours
I loved one and favoured it the most.
It was much larger than the other marbles
And could be pointed easily out
Colour of the marble like the iris of an eye
Used to dazzle if taken in hand
It reflected the glaring of thousand rainbow
Which have just been wash in rain drops.

I have hardly any idea about
When, where and how I lost the marble
In later days, so many coloured marbles
Filled the box
Lest I feel the want of that particular marble
And it gives me a faint pain inside.

The train started moving gradually
Leaving far behind the rural platform
It aimed at the city strange and unknown
Which is bound in concrete
The smoke filled with steam came out of his breast

Blurred the terminal station too
And it wetted the two eyes
Watching outside the windows.

Paddy fields, lakes of lotus flowers
Woodnotes of doves
Slowly all disappeared;
Though their shadows become visible
Leaning against the horizon of the sky far away
Every often so
Where the river Hooghly meets.

That was my first experience boarding a plane
The nature perhaps poured all her tears during that entire
night
As I was about to leave my city,
Dew, my daughter of eleven months.
Taming thousands of questions and perplexity in her eyes
Dew gazed at me,
I hurriedly had touched her hand
And got into the cab.

Her mama standing by the door
Holding Dew in lap
The photo still blazes
In the album of my memory.
Those photos black and white

Left behind long ago
Are conserved in my mind
With great care
I crave not to forget them ever.

One coming day perhaps
The canvas would whiten gradually
All these photos
Would be erased from my memory ;

So before that day knocks at the door
I turn the leaves of the memory album
For one more time.

51. I Have Altered Myself A Great Deal

Longing to get you back
I have altered myself a great deal
Setting aside all my weird petulance and indiscipline
I have adopted civil gentility.

My life moves now with the stern instruction of clock
Like the clerics of nine to five
I obey all the conventional rules when I work.
You don't have to worry anymore-
I'll not raise you from slumber
Before the cracking of dawn
To show the magic of changing of colour
Of the lotus plant that grows on land
At the neighbouring bower.
Or
Never visit your office on an over-fraught day
Out of the blue
To show you rainbow
At the sky of Maidan
After a shower of rain,
You will never have to listen to
The sound of blooming of the autumn flower

At the dead of night.

You will be overjoyed to know
That I, like a materialistic man of middle income group
Accumulate cash each and every month
In the savings account
I have a plan to take you
To a dream city abroad
during the pujas, next year.

Who knows-perhaps
Bunch of Rhododendron changes its hue in that city
Icy lake dazzles with thousands of rainbows
In the first beam of the sun
And slumber cracks at midnight
With the tiptoeing of snowfall.

You don't have to worry anymore-I have altered myself a great
deal
Only to gain you back
In my life.

52. My Funeral

The hall is enormously large
Silent, hushed and quiet
Brimming with crowd is the hall
I saw them all to carefully skulk
They are vigilantly sharing their views but in whisper.

A table is nicely decorated
And laid at the corner of the hall
A large photograph bound in a frame is kept at the centre
It is fraught with jasmine
A bunch of joysticks spread splendid perfume standing in
front.

The photograph is of none other than mine
It has been collected with much difficulty.
I had ever been shy to a cam
I am clad in dhoti and kurta in this photograph
That had been taken from a play
Where I acted an elderly uncle.

Song of Tagore is been played
It has a low pace, and tells of some sad tale
The song is appropriate for the melancholy environment.

Then came a few chosen orators
All they are quite close friends
They ruminated over some of their fond memories with me.

I really loved to hear from them
They uttered kind words
And gave appraisal to my deeds
They reminisced some of my behaviours
That disgusted them about me
But it is really a miracle that
How one's misconduct
Becomes a food for laughter as one departs !

Is there anyone in heaven or earth
Who does not enjoy listening his own applaud -
So I have thrown a funeral party
Before I die.

I am quite well
Not in need for flowers, joysticks
And more appropriating the occasion.

I despise melancholy songs of lesser pace
And have prepared my own playlist.
At the beginning there will be the song of
Inseparable friendship

From the movie 'Sholay'
This follows 'Part Time Lover' by Stevie Wonder.
The list will end in
That eternal song by Manna De
'Jakhan keu amake pagol bale'
(when someone calls me crazy).

I crave to spend a single day
With my friends
I planned to avail myself
All the fun and celebrate my being on this planet.

Hence all you are cordially invited
To my funeral party.

53. Contrivances For Writing Poetry

Sir, you have sought
The perfect shop for your purpose
Our shop is fraught with
The contrivances for making modern poetry.
We shall guide you with all our knowledge
The contrivances those are most relevant,
And which have become obsolete.

For instance
River, cloud and rain you do not
Need to buy
Purchasing these will be a great loss
To your fund
Public do not care about all these
Nowadays anymore.

If you pick up
Birds and flowers
Go for the non-native ones
Peculiar and bizarre exotic names
Get a cordial reception.
Days are gone for jasmine, lotus and Siuli.

Politics, murk and mire
Have an inordinate demand;
On the contrary
Don't drench your verses
With grief, despondency and melancholia
Sere utterance of these words will be devastating
Nobody likes to deal with all these
What did you say ?

Love, warmth, passion and languishments?
You'll get into a great danger boss !
It will drive you out of your hospice,
Your readers will simply send you to a loony - bin.

Instead, I am providing you with
A blend of hatred, loathing and abhorrence
And an umpteen of some grudge, malevolence and venom
Newly imported from abroad.

Now you make a list
And tell me what items would you like to buy ?

54. Home Address Unremembered

I am too late in getting back
Years melted in other years
Bringing homely beauty to my life
The address of my home I lost.

It was easy to get back home
Through the dykes of my known fields,
Pitch cast broad roadways
Move through rending cloud of the sky
They hardly care about
The address where my home lie.

Once there was a marshy land
Now concrete boasts its dominion
Headstrong concrete and sand
Do not care of our union.

The mango plants and its petty neighbour
Were happy to direct my home
As they spread their stems and dour
Near the map of my sweet dome.
Now with oppression of brick

All they succumbed
Few are fallen apart sick
And they all are now dumb.

• 134 •

Few loved ones were there
Waiting for my reach
Now they are no more near
Quite they out of pitch.

I am too late in getting back home
My heart is still love laden
But I found only four walls had come
All other had forsaken.

A pain to my breast I felt
As no beloved to welcome me had left.

55. Anticipation

You may come to me now
You need not have to worry
I shall not burden thou
With my despair and sorrow.

Crons of my despair
Were being sun baked
Upon the smooth patio overlaid with cow dung
Do not know when
Pigeons ate them all.

You don't need to compromise anymore
Deluge of Ajay washed
My love unfathomable unprecedented.
My sole self too had gone crossing the shore.

I am a derelict now
I have left with no love and no sorrow
Long for you
What all I do
Cause now I've come to know
I won't get you unless I give in and everything I flow.

www.ingramcontent.com/pod-product-compliance
Lightning Source LLC
Chambersburg PA
CBHW021543150726
47990CB00006B/2376